How to Be Productive Working at Home:
101 Productivity Hacks

Deb Gilbert

Copyright © 2014, Deb Gilbert
ALL RIGHTS RESERVED
Cover Design © 2014 pro_ebookcovers
http://www.gilbertedservices.com

All rights reserved. No part of this publication or the author's website may be reproduced or transmitted in any form or by any means, including informational storage and retrieval systems, without explicit written permission from the author or publisher, except for brief quotations in a review.

Disclaimer: Although the author and publisher have made every effort to ensure that the information in this book was correct at press time, the author and publisher do not assume and hereby disclaim any liability to any party for any loss, damage, or disruption caused by errors or omissions, whether such errors or omissions result from negligence, accident, or any other cause.

ISBN-13: 978-1512375749
ISBN-10: 1512375748

This book is dedicated to all of us who work from home. Three cheers for telecommuters!

CONTENTS

INTRODUCTION..VII
CHAPTER 1: TIME MANAGEMENT TIPS TO GET THINGS DONE............1
CHAPTER 2: ESTABLISHING WORK ROUTINES...7
CHAPTER 3: BLOCKING OUT DISTRACTIONS..13
CHAPTER 4: ORGANIZING YOUR SCHEDULE AND WORK SPACE.......17
CHAPTER 5: PRODUCTIVITY TOOLS..23
CHAPTER 6: ENERGY MANAGEMENT..25
CHAPTER 7: MOTIVATION AND LIFESTYLE TIPS..................................29
CONCLUSION...37
ABOUT THE AUTHOR..39
ENDNOTES...41

INTRODUCTION

DOES WORKING FROM HOME REALLY RAISE PRODUCTIVITY?

In a recent study by Nicholas Bloom and his student at the Harvard Business School, Bloom mentioned that the participants (the staff at Ctrip call center) were happier and more productive working at home.[1] This is compared to those who still worked from their office. Another study done by Stanford University researchers supports this idea. About 13,000 workers from one company had higher feelings of work satisfaction working from home.[2]

I work from home, and I know that just like any work-at-home individual that being productive does not happen each day. Despite all the research articles stating there is a relationship of working at home and getting more things done, you (and I) do not wake up every day feeling enthusiastic to finish tasks.

When I quit my day job as a curriculum specialist, I had several online schools in which I was teaching. My first two weeks of working from home were rather strange. First, I had not thought about when I would work, so I started the day with the morning news and then I would find myself flipping through channels and Tivo for something to watch. When TV no longer entertained me, I did housework, and I generally walked around the house wondering what to do. I would go to the mall and walk and shop. In the evening, I would do my work on my laptop while watching television. This was not productive, and it was stressful. What I

---

1 http://hbr.org/2014/01/to-raise-productivity-let-more-employees-work-from-home/ar/1

2 http://web.stanford.edu/~nbloom/WFH.pdf

finally did was to evaluate my situation and made a plan that led me to more work and less time doing it.

Working at home, or telecommuting, calls for more self-discipline. Unlike working in an office where the course for the day is already set out for you, working from home has some unique distractions. Sometimes, the weather's calling you to go outside, or your kids are asking for more playtime. Perhaps your friend calls and wants to head out shopping. These interruptions, I think, are the prime challenges for anyone who works from home.

The phrase, "home is the most comfortable place to work," does not always apply. We may think in terms of no screaming boss, no dress code, and no short breaks; however, there is more to working at home and being productive. The truth is there are a multitude of distractions inside the house. However, as a freelancer, you cannot allow any distractions cause you to miss deadlines or have irate clients.

This book, which I dedicate to you, is a work of the heart to give you more insights on being productive while working at home. This book includes more than 30 productivity tools and more than 100 productivity hacks. It is a collection of the best productivity hacks every successful home-based worker needs to know. I hope you have a great time reading and using my tips!

CHAPTER 1: TIME MANAGEMENT TIPS TO GET THINGS DONE

Time is a telecommuter's best resource. Many of us fight to have more time, believing that it is a battle where more time can be had. However, we all have the same 24 hours in a day, and some people tend to become more productive than others.[3] It is amazing how some of us manage a house with five children while working at home. Some of us even have other gigs aside from our home-based jobs. The answer can be summarized in two words: **time management.**

Keeping yourself in the loop is the first thing you have to consider as a telecommuter. You will have many challenges along the way, and most of them will usually stem from improper time management. Maybe you are having a difficult time setting deadlines and experimenting with a workable schedule. As someone who works from home as an online professor, I still experiment with my schedule. I make sure to make the most of my precious time despite some inconsistencies. Many freelancers would say that rhythm is the key to getting things done. If you have a volume of projects with different deadlines, it will be challenging to stick to one agenda. Here are some surefire ways to manage your time efficiently and be more productive:

START MEASURING YOUR PRODUCTIVITY AND TIME. Some say it is difficult to change what you without some data, so the first step is to track the time you[4] spend on the computer. There are masses of time-tracking apps and software out there for you to try. Harvest is a time-tracking and billing app in which you can view from a desktop or mobile phone. This web-based app comes with a free-trial and basic plans if you want more features. In case you are looking for a user-centered tool, you may try Everhour. It is free for individuals and offers simple pricing for a team. For measuring time you spend on your phone, use aTimeLogger. It is a smartphone app for iOS and Android users. This app helps keeps track of every activity. RescueTime is another useful application if you want to monitor how long you spend on the computer. Eternity Time Log Lite is another app that tracks time while managing various clients.

STOP PROCRASTINATING. I often find myself thinking more than doing more. It is one form of procrastination. Unless you do deliberate thinking, stop thinking about the things you want to do, and start doing them now. There are times when I procrastinate, and then I just try to finish what I have to do and no more. It really does not feel right. Whenever I feel like I am procrastinating too much, I try to remember Parkinson's Law.[5] It says, "Work expands so as to fill the time available for its completion." Remember, procrastinating can be paralyzing. Thus, we all need to have the willpower to break the procrastination cycle.[6]

COMPLETE A TASK ONE AT A TIME. As the saying goes, "If you chase two rabbits, both will escape." The bottom line here is to focus. Working on a single project at a time gives you a much better chance of completing it. Multitasking is okay, but it can be harmful. Doing two or three things at the same time surely give could result in low-quality outputs. There was a time when I tried multitasking with my projects, but then as I was warned, I was challenged in producing quality work. I was bombarded with too much information, and it slowed me down. Lesson learned. Do it one at a time. I will add a caveat here. Multitasking menial work like saving files, Facebook reads, and personal email are not included here. This one- task-at-a-time thing is for your important-needs-to-be-perfect projects.

PRIORITIZE. What task is the most important task of all? It is time to adjust your focus. Decide what is worth your time. Knowing how to prioritize can be the best productivity hack as there are times when we cannot get things done because we do not place them in order of importance. If you find yourself spending half of your day on the not crucial things like playing video games or spending too much time watching TV, you will only feel guilty later for not doing the most important things. Prioritizing means knowing what matters most to you, and that is most important for any successful entrepreneur to know. Setting priorities is the spiritual secret to increasing productivity. I use the sticky notes on Windows 8 to set my daily schedule in order of importance. I, usually, do this the night before. When I start my day, I have a pink sticky note that shows me what I need to do in order of importance with deadlines added.

We all have several goals. It can be a lifetime goal or just the goals you want to do daily. Whatever it is, it will help to write them down. Write a list of everything you want to accomplish in life. Based on that list, identify them based on their qualities using four quadrants: important and urgent; important and semi-urgent; important and not urgent; and not important or urgent.

SET UP A ROUTINE. You already know that I had had inconsistencies when it came to work schedules. However, I often start my work in the afternoon. I am a night owl and late riser. My peak performance time is after 6 pm. That's when my brain is ready to pound out some work. Many people, unlike me, appreciate the silence in the morning when they can just drink their coffee and dive straight into work. There are times when it might be a good idea to work while everybody's still asleep. If you are a work-at-home mom, you might find it easy to work when the children are asleep or napping. On the few days that I do rise early, I do like to know that after four hours or so, I am free to do whatever I choose.

MAKE USE OF AUTOCORRECT FEATURES AND HOTKEYS. These can help you save time editing your work. There are a lot of keyboard shortcuts to learn, depending on the software you use. For example, you can use the Alt-tab key in switching tabs. Want to underline words and not spaces? Use control + shift + w if you're using a PC and command + shift + w if you're on Mac. It is just one of many shortcuts you can use.[7] Better, use your spare time learning the keyboard commands for your PC or MAC. There are plenty of YouTube tutorials for keyboard shortcuts. CNet's Executive Editor Tom Merritt came up with 15 Best Keyboard Shortcuts video on YouTube. You may want to use Nuance's Dragon Naturally Speaking as I do. I find that once the software is trained, I can dictate my feedback to students quite quickly. I also use it to write books. There is an app for your iPhone, as well.

LIMIT YOUR TIME DOING RESEARCH ON THE INTERNET. Too much screen time is eye-straining and time consuming. I often commit this mistake of spending too much time on my research. Sometimes, I even find myself being hooked in one article or site that I forget my original task. Whenever that happens, I just bookmark the page for later-viewing. For instances like this, you can use an app which reminds you of tasks. Try Remember the Milk. It makes it convenient to be reminded to stay on task. Taskos Task List is another reminder app for Android, which has a clean presentation and easy-to-navigate feature.

LIVE BY THE TWO-MINUTE RULE. Whenever you think a task is easy that it can be done in just two minutes, go ahead and do it. David Allen emphasized this technique in his book Get Things Done.[8] This two-minute rule also works for writers like me. In two minutes, I can write a sentence or two and later on, I might find myself writing for an hour using that idea. I put my idea on a sticky note. As a telecommuter, this two-minute rule applies to me in so many ways like replying to email, for example. What else you can do under two minutes? File a paper, empty the trash can, check the calendar, text your son.

REMIND YOURSELF ABOUT DEADLINES. They say there are two important acts for any worker: make time and set deadlines. Calendar apps are great, but sometimes you need to track how many days you still have for certain projects. Any.DO is a free app which can work as a time manager and a to-do list. Whatever app you use to monitor deadlines, it is necessary to be realistic and not too ambitious. Give yourself some time away from the project so you can return to it with new eyes.

AUTO-PAY YOUR BILLS. It can save you so much time. Just setup direct deposits to make sure you have enough money in your accounts. In Ireland, there's what they call Get It Keep It, which covers all providers such as electricity, landline, and cable TV. In the US, all you have to do is set up Bill Pay with your bank. Once it is set up, schedule your payment dates in your agenda or on a sticky note, and pay during a two-minute task period.

SHOP ONLINE. Instead of going to the store, take advantage of online stores and place your orders online. Nowadays, online shops carry free shipping and sell almost all items you can think of. According to the Oprah website, some of the best online grocery sites are Anson Mills, Red Truck Bakery, and Market Hall Foods. For home products, there's All Modern and Circa Lighting. For clothing and accessories, some of the top choices by many are Bluefly, Way Fair, and HauteLook. My favorite is Amazon.com. I like it because it is fast and with the Prime Shipping feature, there are no shipping charges after the initial $79 payment. My item comes in two days, and I have time to do some prime 'me' shopping when I head for the mall or the boutiques. I just ordered some sink liners online, as an example. I found some decorative mats and do not have to worry about buying the more mundane things during my shopping expeditions.

SET A TIME LIMIT ON MEETINGS. If it is just an information-sharing type of meeting, it is a must to set limits for you to save time. However, if you are in a special meeting with a client where you need to discuss a project or conduct brainstorming, do not hurry. The client needs your quality time. Just learn to categorize meetings based on their importance. Some meetings will allow you to do the multitasking that I warned you about above. As a freelancer, I have many meetings that I must attend online. I go to the web meeting and listen while doing two-minute tasks here and there.

USE THE PARETO TECHNIQUE. You may use this technique to your advantage. Pareto is about focusing on the input (time, resources, and effort) to achieve the output (results, rewards, and revenue). It is also called the 80/20 rule. The 20 percent goes to the input while the remaining 80 goes to the output. [9]

Truly, we cannot stop time, but there are many things we can do to utilize time efficiently. Do you find yourself struggling with time management? If so, what can you do to resolve the issue? I hope you found useful information from this chapter. The next chapter will include work routines, an important factor in boosting productivity.

CHAPTER 2: ESTABLISHING WORK ROUTINES

Working from home is a dream job for many employees. Unless you come up with proper routines before you engage in your work, your dream job will turn into a nightmare. Setting up rituals also helps in automating behaviors. Productive people have a personal system they follow every single day. They have routines to keep them going. Besides, work routines are great ways to meet goals on a daily basis. Almost everyone who works from home has a routine before getting to work. There are some of us who write every morning at 3 am. There are some who schedule their meals and work out sessions. While our routines depend on the kind of lifestyle that we want to have, it will not hurt to try these tips:

USE MORNINGS TO FOCUS ON YOURSELF. Successful entrepreneurs like Jeff Imelt and Indra Nooyi use mornings to seize the day. They ignore emails, read the news, take showers, and eat a full breakfast.[10] When we were kids, we were taught not to skip breakfast. It makes sense now that we are adults because skipping breakfast can ruin many hours of our productivity. What other things can you do to focus on yourself in the morning? Consider not checking emails in the morning. You have to control email before it controls you. No productive person will tell you to spend more time on emails. Research suggests that checking email frequently drops one's IQ to 10 points.[11] So rather than hurrying up to turn on the computer and check emails, focus on yourself first. Having an opening ritual, which is dedicated to your first eases both the mind and the body.

WORK WHEN THE HOUSE IS NICE AND QUIET. Wife onboard or kids onboard? Without either of the two, some people still find it hard to work even if they have a dedicated space for work. I know someone, a work-at-home dad and scriptwriter, who works while the kids are at school. Of course, if your family members can understand your job, you can communicate with them that you are working. I live alone, so my house is quiet all the time. When I travel and have friends and family around, I ask for a TV tray and chair in my room so I can close the door and get some work done. I have heard of parents putting up signs on their office doors, only to have every family member ignore it. Have a talk to your family and see if you can work out a way to avoid distractions with their help.

SLEEP ON TIME AND GET UP ON TIME. Babies need to sleep on time and get up on time for them to get used to their sleeping routines. The experts say adults need the same. Sleeping better and smarter is one way to establish a healthy routine. One study suggests that lack of good sleep can shrink one's brain.[12] Sleeping better can be done in so many ways and here are some tips to help give you better snooze time:

- Lessen screen time. Checking your email or watching TV before bedtime lessens your chance of having a good night sleep. So keep the phone and laptop out of reach and turn off the TV.[13]

- Get rid of "buzzer" type alarms. A buzzer alarm clock is annoying. While alarm clocks wake you up easily, waking up with its sound feels like being attacked. If you still need an alarm clock to wake you up, just go for music and not the buzzer type. I use my iPhone alarm that links to my favorite music.

- Add an extra hour of sleep. We make mistakes when we get tired. We become less-able to produce quality work. Do you sleep

four to six hours only at night? If possible, add an extra hour of sleep every night so you can recharge more.
- Start your day at least an hour earlier. Waking up earlier than usual gives you time to charge your batteries and gain clarity on your priorities. They say most successful people start their day before sunrise. Studies also suggest that mornings can either make or break your day. I tried getting up a little earlier than the usual and I was surprised how an hour makes me complete a couple extra tasks. Just imagine, being finished with your main agenda items in the late morning. For me, this gives me a great excuse for a nap or exercise.
  - Get energized. Even if you are task-oriented, it is not easy to work when the bed is calling you to curl up and take a nap. Then there are times when you want to work after lunch, but the afternoon slump is hard to beat. According to Chantalle Gerber's article in Tiny Buddha, laziness is a natural part of life but it has the potential to consume us.[14] Here are some tricks to jumpstart your brain and get things done:
  - Listen to music. Dr. Teresa Lesiuk, an assistant professor for music therapy at the University of Miami, conducted a research on the importance of music at the workplace. Dr. Lesiuk found out that those who listened to music completed their tasks more quickly than their counterparts who did not.[15] So, whenever you need music to wake you up, grab your earphones and tune in music. If you are anxious and stressed out, try listening to soothing music. I have a great portable speaker system that I use with my iTunes on my iPhone.
  - Have a little burst of caffeine. In a survey conducted by Harris Interactive in 2011, it showed that 46% of employees claim of being less-productive without coffee.[16] If you belong to the club of coffee lovers, just limit your caffeine to two or three

cups a day. That is a safe number, according to the Department of Health.

- • Crank out some exercises. Do not have time to hit the gym? It is time to learn about office-friendly exercises or "deskercise" as they call it. Emily Milam of Greatist.com came up with 33 Smart Ways to Exercise at Work. Some examples are the Desk Chair swivel, The Fab Abs Squeeze, and the Posture Perfecter. Put a small pedal machine under your desk and pedal or set up a treadmill with a laptop.
- Take a power nap. A 10-minute power nap does not just boost productivity. It also sharpens focus. Do you want to master power nap? Perfecting a great daytime snooze is not challenging at all. Just pick the perfect time and make sure to have a comfortable place to lie down. Keep your naps between 10 and 30 minutes. Have an alarm set so you will not end up in a deep sleep or REM sleep. Napping longer than that will make you groggy and not energized.

DO REAL WORK. Working from home does not mean you are not working anymore. Respect your work even if there is no boss watching you. If you think you cannot do real work with your iPad, maybe it is time to switch back to a desktop or laptop. I do my best work in my office with two extra monitors. The three screens help me with being able to see documents while writing in Word, and the third screen may have email up.

HAVE SOME SPIRITUAL TIME. In a talk given by Ratnaghosha, a member of the Triratna Buddhist Order said that individual productivity is related to one's spiritual practice. When it comes to productivity blogs, one of my top picks is Zen Habits. The posts do not just talk about being productive. It also talks about one's personal being and other important life issues like dealing with relationships and developing selfless compassion. For most employees, spiritual maturity leads to better working. Before your day begins, thank God for the wisdom. Ask Him to help you stay focused. More importantly, establish a closing ritual and that could be through a prayer, too.

For some, routines are easy. For me, they are extremely mind-numbing—it is not exciting to do the same thing every day at the same time. For people who really take organization as a serious matter, routine is very essential. I feel there is a happy medium in which I can be very productive, and the incentive is that I can end my work period early.

I like what novelist Pearl S. Buck said about routines. Quoting her, she said "I don't wait for moods. You accomplish nothing if you do that. Your mind must know it has got to get down to work."

Deb Gilbert

CHAPTER 3: BLOCKING OUT DISTRACTIONS

Distraction is one thing that could hamper not just a freelancer's productivity, but also his creativity. Distraction at home leads to lack of concentration. Working from home, you have to be proactive when it comes to removing distractions because, in this career, you are your own boss. There is no such thing as "distraction-free" zone at home. Nobody will tell you to stop using Facebook, YouTube, or Twitter unless you do it proactively. On average, people who use computer for work are distracted once every 10 and a half minutes.[17] Truly, those addicting websites are the number one distraction for many people.

You sit there in front of your computer, swearing to be productive today. Next thing you know, it is at the eleventh hour, and you are still browsing your favorite websites. For some, doing anything work-related when you stay at home is the hardest thing to do. If you find it difficult to avoid distraction, remember to "concentrate on concentrating." Hence, here are some tips you can try to get rid of anything that will pull you away from the task at hand.[18]

TURN OFF THE TV. Watching TV is another black hole while working from home. An average American watches TV at least 34 hours a week. Just imagine how much work can be done in 34 hours. You could have used that time to relax after a long day of work or read a good book, or get your job done!

CLOSE UNNECESSARY TABS. Multiple web browsers open on the desktop is another form of distraction. Close tabs and windows that are not work-related. Having many tabs open at once does not just make the browser unstable and slow, it also suggests unproductivity as one could have a hard time focusing on the immediate task at hand. Chrome has a feature which consolidates all your tabs into one. You can utilize this feature if you do not want to open too many tabs. I time myself. I give myself five minutes of Facebook games each hour. Sometimes, I forget to use this incentive, but I feel the distraction does help in the end. In an office environment, people will stop by your desk and chat or you will go to the vending machine. At home, I try to forget the refrigerator and reward myself with a few games of Bejeweled Blitz.

SWITCH OFF YOUR PHONE. It is the biggest distraction. If you are not using iPhone and cannot switch it off, better switch it in Do Not Disturb mode. This feature in iOS 7 and 8 turns off sounds and vibrates. Moreover, do not it answer phone calls unless it is a work-related call.

ELIMINATE UNNECESSARY EMAILS. Doing that, you will not need to spend time reading unimportant messages. Or if possible, just set a specific time for checking emails, like doing it every 2pm or every 7pm only. This is more efficient than reading or answering emails all day long. Some of you will need to check work email often. This is when I find the use of multiple monitors a plus.

TUNE OUT THE NEWS. Most of the time, nothing important really happens. What do we often hear from news? Crimes, poverty, and war. If daily news is giving you information overload, it is time to tune out. The point here is not to make people "news illiterate." The issue here is to stop watching news if you think that is distracting.

BLOCK ONLINE ADS. Admit it– online ads are annoying. These online ads do not just add to the screen clutter; they kill our productivity by preventing us from focusing on what we need to read or research online. They also increase the loading time of various sites. The easiest thing to do is to install a free Adblock Plus plugin to disable malware domains and social media buttons on certain websites—be sure to check out the documentation.

AVOID THE URGE TO GO ONLINE. List down all the websites you visit often and block them using browser extensions. It is not complicated to do as there are hundreds of site-blocking apps and online tools out there that you may use. Concentrate is a nice option if you want to launch tools you need to complete your activity and quit apps which are unnecessary. For example, once you activate "writing," you will be blocked to Facebook, Twitter, and the like while automatically launching Microsoft Word. On the contrary, Dejal- Time Out is another app which lets you take regular breaks. It is a good reminder so you can relax and rebuild your energy. These apps are available for Mac. For PC users, Freedom and Dark Room (for writers) are some of the site-blocking apps I know.

TRY THE POMODORO TECHNIQUE. The aim of this technique is to increase the user's focus. It is best for people who are distracted very easily (it is easy to be distracted at home). This works by breaking down a big task into smaller subtasks. Let's say you have 25 minutes to focus on a selected task. Try to work on one thing as hard as you can without any distraction. Once Pomodoro is completed, you can now reward yourself with a short break. Wikipedia-wise, Pomodoro is Italian for tomato. A tomato-shaped timer was initially used for this technique. If you want a tool which works exactly like this technique, just download Strict Workflow (be logged into Chrome for this one). This tool blocks certain pages while you work. A click on the tomato simply starts the timer. Like the Pomodoro technique, you will also have a five-minute break after completing a task.[19]

PICK YOUR BATTLES. Do not waste your precious time getting bogged down in trivial battles. Fight for the important battles. Think of all the things you have to do and make sure to spend your time more on the important ones than just the urgent ones.

What distracts you? Identify your time wasters and get rid of them. Whenever you feel like you are out of focus, just remember what Winston Churchill once said: "You will never reach your destination if you stop and throw stones at every dog that barks."

CHAPTER 4: ORGANIZING YOUR SCHEDULE AND WORK SPACE

Staying organized in every aspect of life is very essential. Without organization, it is tough to identify how to start doing things and how to deal with all of life's chaos. Finding a system for everything is an important factor in getting things done. Organizing comes with many benefits. It reduces stress and clutter; it saves time and money; and it makes us more efficient in our work. Being organized is one of the first things to keep in mind if you want to be more productive. Here are some organization tips you may apply as a home-based worker:

UNDERSTAND THAT YOU HAVE TO START…..AND KEEP STARTING. As a writer, one of my biggest fears is starting something. However, I realized that I will never feel success if I do not start. Let me quote Buddha for his opinion about starting something. He said, "There are two mistakes one can make along the road to truth…not going all the way and not starting."

KEEP YOUR TO-DO LISTS SEPARATE. Create separate lists of your tasks for work and for household chores. This works especially for moms. If you want to master your to-do list, it is important that you find the right tool for writing down your task. A simple notepad will do or your sticky notes, but I bet you will really like an electronic noting system such as Evernote and Google Keep. It makes sense to go paperless; you can check on your notes wherever you are.

SEPARATE YOUR WORKPLACE FROM FAMILY SPACE. It is the same as setting aside time for work and family. There should be a boundary even if you are working from home. Make sure you do not think about the office when you are in your family space, and do not think about family when you are at your home office.

Set deadlines. As you meet a deadline cross it off as completed. This gives you a sense of accomplishment afterwards. The importance of setting deadlines is that it prevents an overloaded work schedule. Deadlines also come with plenty of benefits. That includes making one more disciplined at work. Whenever you find it challenging to set deadlines, just remember this one-liner, "Goals are dreams with deadlines."

DIVIDE AND CONQUER. The divide-and-conquer technique has been used for ages. It is time to beat the chaos of doing so many tasks at once. Batch similar things altogether and do them at once.

WRITE IT DOWN. Sometimes, pen and paper will have a therapeutic effect. Write down everything you want to get done, everything you need to get done, and everything you would like to do. Then you will have to categorize these things and assign the time when you can do them. It is an effective technique to help you prioritize. Meanwhile, jotting things down will help you remember the things you have to do. As soon as you think of a task, jot it downright away. [20] I often make a grocery list only to leave it at home. More times than not, however, I remember the contents of that list because I did write it down.

CREATE A PHYSICAL WORKSPACE. Though you can work anywhere inside the house or out, it will help to create a physical workspace. In fact, the office space is one of the five most important factors in feeling professionally happy.[21] The others are task choices, learning opportunities, work relationships, and your schedule. It does not have to be traditional where there are book racks or magazine racks. If you have a really small space at home, you do not have to try to fit in all these things. Just aim for good lighting and proper desk and chair. If you already have a dedicated space for work, it is time to declutter it. Do not worry; it only takes an extra 10 minutes to declutter your workspace. If you do not already have one, here are other tips for setting up an office space.

AIM FOR NATURAL LIGHTING. If you cannot place your desk near a window or anywhere you can get natural light, use an adjustable light like a small lamp.

ASSOCIATE THE RIGHT TOUCH OF COLORS ON YOUR WORK DESK. Blue, red, yellow, and white are great choices. Blue helps increase productivity while stimulating the mind. If you are doing analytics work then blue is the best choice. For those who do physical work, then red is the right color to increase one's energy. Red also stimulates breathing and heart rate. For those who often do creative work, use more of yellow. Yellow, an optimistic color, inspires and increases one's concentration. Meanwhile, if you are that "jack of all trade" type of freelancer, white will be the best option. Just imagine how this color reflects light and create an open, airy feeling.[22]

ADD A PERSONAL TOUCH ON YOUR WORK SPACE. Add some photos or desk toys on your desk. This will make you more motivated and inspired to do your work. Once you are comfortable with your working space, there is a better chance for you to come up with quality work.

WRITE DOWN YOUR GOALS. At the end of each workday, I always check if I accomplished at least three of my goals for that day. Of course, there are days when one or even three are not accomplished. However, when all of them are completed, it gives me a sense of triumph. Isn't it nice when you met all of your goals, no matter how small or big they are? They say seeing your goals on a paper create a powerful effect on the mind. Meanwhile, I like this "Goals Pyramid" I got from WriteMarketDesign.com. The pyramid begins with a primary goal. Let's say you want to publish a book. From that, you have to identify the initial steps you have to do to accomplish your primary goal. Based from the example, you have to outline and research. Next is to come up with things you have to do every day, every week, and every month. To sum it up, be specific in writing down your goals. List down every single detail of what you want.

SET EXCITING GOALS. After you write down your goals, the question is: Did you have any of them that excited you? If not, why not try setting exciting goals for yourself? That way, you will be more inspired to work.

CAPTURE ALL CREATIVE IDEAS. Creativity can make one happier. Whenever I find something creative, whether it is an image or an article, I save it for later viewing. For saving files like articles, videos, and photos, Instapaper is a web app that you can try. Or, if you just want to write down stuff, Evernote is a great option.

LEARN TO SAY NO. You do not have to respond to everyone or everything. Learn to ignore things that do not matter. The problem with most of us is that we always say yes when someone asks us to do something. When somebody asks you to do something that is time consuming or something you rather not do, there is always a polite way to say no.

KEEP ALL YOUR FILES IN ONE PLACE. For saving files, I use Dropbox. It also serves as an automatic backup of important files whenever I am on the go. For saving sensitive info like credit card number and passwords, try LockBox. Google Drive is an easy-to-use web-based office app. This app makes it easy to collaborate with co-freelancers or clients, as well as share files with them. Google Drive's Docs, Forms, and Spreadsheets are all user-friendly.

PLAN AHEAD. According to How to Master Your Time author Brian Tracy, you will save 10 minutes for every minute you spend planning.[23] Given that, I usually start the week with a planning session. Sunday evenings are the perfect time to plan for a week. I always have my planner with me where I list down at least three to five small goals that I have to accomplish each day. Google Calendar, like Cozi, is an ideal tool for sharing information with your family members. You can always adjust the list at your nightly planning meeting with yourself.

SPEED UP YOUR INTERNET. The need for speed is crucial in every business, even in small ones. Use a fast and reliable broadband if possible. Trust me on this—it is worth it.

ELIMINATE CLUTTER AND PILES OF PAPER ON YOUR WORK DESK. Clutter will lead you to dislike your work space. Piles of paper may go unnoticed for weeks, but just think how nice it would be to have a nice clean and orderly workspace.

DO PRODUCTIVE PROCRASTINATION. You cannot help but take breaks. You deserve a break. There are things you can do during breaks which count as productive. Go running or walking or run an errand. Or perhaps, organize your work space!

START DELEGATING. You do not have to do everything on your own. If there is anyone else who can help you, then make use of this resource.[24] Sharing responsibility is part of getting a job done smarter. Delegating tasks can be done not just in the workplace, but also can be done in personal tasks you do not have time for such as household chores. If the kids can handle household chores, ask them to help you out and do the things they can do for themselves. You may want to consider about childcare if you have small children. Use Fiverr for some low-cost help for the more menial tasks. Do not waste your time doing things other people can do. Seek help when you need it. If you cannot say no, just delegate the things you do not want to do or those that are not on the top of your priority list. Some outsourcing sites you can try are ScriptLance (Freelancer), Guru, eLance, and GetFriday.

COMPLETE WHAT WAS LEFT UNDONE FROM THE PREVIOUS DAY. Sometimes, the hardest thing to do is complete an unfinished task from yesterday. To make it easier to manage tasks, try Wunderlist. It is a not-so-complicated app for organizing and completing tasks. It looks like a simpler version of Evernote.

STICK TO YOUR SCHEDULE. Creating a schedule is as easy as 1-2-3. Sticking to it is another problem. I mentioned this earlier, and I swear it is one of the hardest things to do. When it comes to sticking to schedule, I learned that it is best to come up with a realistic schedule so it will be easy to follow. Sometimes, we try to squeeze a week's worth of tasks into two days. Avoid doing this so you will not end up disappointed afterwards.

CLEAR EMAIL INBOXES AT THE END OF THE DAY. Keeping the inbox clean is one way to organize. Respond to important emails and delete the junk ones.

Richard Branson once said, "I have always lived my life making lists: lists of people to call, lists of ideas, lists of companies to set up, lists of people who can make things happen. Each day I work through these lists, and that sequence of calls moves me forward." Writing down all your tasks will give you an idea how much you need to do.[25]

There is no single precise way to organize. What matters most is how organizing makes your life less complicated. After all, being organized does not mean you are aiming for perfection. It is a system to simplify and destress your life.

CHAPTER 5: PRODUCTIVITY TOOLS

Years ago, the only available tools were pen and paper. These tools are still the best for me at times, but I feel very lucky to have technology. There are thousands of apps and devices we can utilize to get things done. This is a great place to get the latest productivity apps for iPhone http://www.lifehack.org/articles/productivity/the-lifehack-big-list-50-top-productivity-apps-for-iphone.html

Everybody needs different tools. Some are happy with journals, some with yellow legal pads, and some with the latest apps that are on the cutting edge. Productivity tools are certainly helpful at business and at home. Here are some recommended approaches and software to try:

KEEP A PEN AND PAPER IN HANDY. Whenever I have something on my head like a task, a simple thought, or just any idea, it makes me feel relieved to write it down.

MAP OUT ALL THE THINGS YOU NEED TO DO. Trello keeps track of projects and deadlines. This tool applies the Kanban approach, which means "organizing the chaos that surrounds" and "uncovering workflow and process problems." Doing these, one will focus on the flow of working. [26]

KEEP AN APP WHICH AUTOMATICALLY SYNCS TO ALL YOUR DEVICES. Cozi is a free tool which can do so many things for you such as using it like your calendar and journal. It is one of the best apps for work-at-home moms as it features a simple family organizer. It also lets you manage shopping and to-do lists while on the go.

USE SITE-BLOCKING APPS AND SOFTWARE. Try Self-Control. This application for Mac will block websites at a certain period of time, or use StayFocusd as a chrome extension. Instead of blocking time-wasting websites, these apps can restrict the amount of time you visit those sites.

Get a tool which lets you visit a website for a number of seconds only. Productivity Owl is a go-to app if you really cannot help but visit those addictive websites. It allows you to visit a webpage before it closes the tabs. There are sites you can still open just by telling the "owl" the allowed websites. Just make sure that they are work-related.

DOCUMENT YOUR PROGRESS. It can be in a journal or on a sticky note. Many freelancers use this technique to avoid procrastination.

Increase your speed. Type faster or read faster. This might sound silly, but this actually helps. Typeracer lets you learn while racing against others. It only takes a few weeks of practice to improve your typing skills. Spreeder is a site if you are interested in learning to read and comprehend faster.

USE IFTTT TO AUTOMATE TASKS. If This Then That works by connecting different web apps together. It is also a nice time-saver. For example, your Google+ status can be posted as your Facebook status. To give you more idea how it works, The PCMAG came up with 100 Best IFTTT recipes.

DOWNLOAD A NOTE-TAKING APP. There are times when our creative juices flow at times and at places we do not expect. Just in case you do not have a notebook and pen with you, it will help to have a note-taking app straight from your phone. For Android users, Swype and Swiftkey are nice tools for easy typing.

TRY WHITE NOISE. If you are the kind of worker who prefers listening to music while working, but find it distracting, you may install White Noise on your Mac or PC. Some of you should prevent music with lyrics as you will tend to focus more on the lyrics of the song, and that could be very distracting.

Productivity tools are just artificial gadgets. Beyond these things, there is something more important. It is being disciplined and motivated, which I will discuss more on the final chapter of this book. The bottom line: Self-discipline is something productivity apps cannot give us.

CHAPTER 6: ENERGY MANAGEMENT

Productivity is about energy and not time. They say the new king to productivity is not really time management but energy management. Thus, it is a must to have a work and life balance in able to preserve the energy we need for the entire day. Creating a boundary between work and life gives you motivation to keep going. Working too much will kill productivity in the long run.[27]

EXERCISE. For some, it may sound like a no-brainer, but exercise helps increase blood flow to the brain. Do yoga or walk. This also gives you some ability to reflect. Whether it is a trip to the gym or a yoga session, it does not just give you an opportunity to reflect, but it also will boost your energy. Doing this will give you a sense of accomplishment afterwards. Some would benefit from getting up and working out before the workday.

PLAN YOUR SLEEP HOURS. They say that if one's sleep hour is random, so are your days. Thus, it helps to come up with a sleep cycle. If you are using iOS, Sleep Time determines sleep efficiency and gives reports of your night sleep. It works by using a sensitive accelerometer which detects movements during the night. Fit Bit is another good investment.

TAKE SMALL AND FREQUENT BREAKS. Whenever I feel like losing my attention span on what I do, I leave the computer and reward myself with a 15-minute break. Whether it is a gardening break or a coffee break, it helps bring back my focus again. It can be as short as five minutes or 10.[28]

KEEP YOUR MIND SHARP. If you want to keep your mind sharp, it helps to exercise both your mind and your body. Believe it or not, some of those time-wasting games do keep our minds sharp.

AVOID STRESS. When we are stressed, our bodies go to a fight-or-flight response. Once the body shifts to this kind of response, we experience a lot of things affecting our bodies. It includes difficulties in swallowing or breathing, need to urinate, and finding it hard to focus or concentrate.

EAT RIGHT. Did you know that productivity is also determined by what you eat? For one to stay bright, it is best to eat right. The best staples are those rich in antioxidants like berries, tomatoes, and green leafy veggies. As much as possible, prevent cholesterol. It slows blood flow to the brain. Instead of indulging with fast-food goodies, eat more salmon and light tuna. They are rich in omega-3 fatty acids.

TAKE NAPS. When your energy runs low, do not hesitate to take a nap. A short 10 to 20-minute nap will not hurt. The best time to take a short nap is from noon to 4 pm.

TAKE A DAY OFF TO CLEAR YOUR HEAD. Whether you work at home or not, you have to step away from things causing you stress. Keep a certain day clear, like "no meeting" day for example. Rejuvenate your mind by following these tips:

EMPTY YOUR MIND. Find a peaceful place where you can desensitize. Then write down everything that clutters your mind such as unfinished tasks, things you want to change, worries about loved ones, and so on. All these things compete for your attention. You must deal with all of these things if you want a clear mind.

BREATHE! First, lie down flat on your back. Then, take a long breath (not a deep one). While doing it, try to relax your shoulders. Do not breathe with your chest. Next is to relax your face, your neck, your jaw, and your cheeks. The last part is to feel the good air entering your lungs.

DITCH PERFECTIONISM. Some things are better done than perfect. In case you have already read The Cult of Done Manifesto, you will learn that it is okay to laugh at perfection. Perfection is boring and will keep you from getting the task done. Try reading the manifesto.

PRACTICE GOOD HABITS. Good habits are the foundation of good time management. If you want to be good at something, do it every day. Starting small is the first thing to do in developing good habits. Changing a habit only takes 66 days.[29] Want to become a good writer? Then write each day.

GET SUPPORT FROM FAMILY OR FRIENDS. It is a must to get support system from people who matter to you. This support we are talking about can be shown even on small things like not distracting you while you work and giving you enough time to rest. Besides, getting sufficient emotional and social support from loved ones will help make your mind sharp. One research shows that getting strong support from family decreases chances of having Alzheimer's disease.

ALLOW SOME SPONTANEITY IF POSSIBLE. Work on a task that motivates you most. Sometimes, people tend to become highly productive when they are motivated to do something.

BE PRESENT IN THE BODY. Being present in the body means to be in tune with your body. Attention and intention are two different things. Maybe some people are just working to pay the bills or get things done because it is needed. That is intentional. However, if you pay attention regarding what you do, you help yourself to become more present in the body. When you give a task your full attention, you have greater chances of producing your best work.

MEDITATE. If you have not tried meditating, perhaps it is time to integrate a new habit into your life. Meditation will help you become mindful of the things around you. Many successful people and entrepreneurs, like Gwyneth Paltrow, Oprah Winfrey, and Steve Jobs practice the art of meditation and mindfulness. For you to practice mindfulness meditation, Helpguide.org came up with four key points: a quiet environment, a point of focus, a comfortable position, and a noncritical attitude. Meditation should be somewhere calm and peaceful. [30]

TAKE A SHOWER. Being clean is proven to boost productivity. Taking a short bath or shower will help refresh your mind and body. Showering with cold water keeps you alert and improves blood circulation.

BE MORE PROACTIVE, LESS REACTIVE. Being proactive is about planning your day and prioritizing. Being reactive is setting yourself up to react on things happening around you. Stephen Covey, author of The 7 Habits of Highly Effective People, defines proactivity as being "in charge of your life, being responsible for it, and tasking actions to master it." [31]

There is a science behind energy management and productivity. Tony Schwartz, the CEO of The Energy Project, says increasing our output harms our productivity. In order to do our best work, we need to restore and rejuvenate our energy throughout the day. Lesson learned: if we push ourselves to continue working during times of low energy, we put our performances in jeopardy. [32]

CHAPTER 7: MOTIVATION AND LIFESTYLE TIPS

When I decided to leave the 'outside' world of work, I never realized how drastic things can be inside the house. There are times when I feel so overwhelmed with so many things to do. There are days when motivational quotes do not inspire me. I end up doing less and leaving more for tomorrow. Then I realized that since I had a lifestyle change, I needed to change my attitude as well.

KEEP A FILE OF POSITIVE FEEDBACK. Whenever you feel stumped or less appreciated, revisit positive feedback from previous clients.

GET IN TOUCH. You might have lost in touch with past colleagues after deciding to work from home. Regardless of that, getting in touch with them is a nice way to relieve your stress.

MAKE THINGS ENJOYABLE. There is so much you can do to make things enjoyable while working from home. Reward yourself with music you like or a favorite snack. Set the mood before you work. It is hard to come up with great results when you feel lazy right before you turn on the laptop, so try to make things more enjoyable.

RELAX. The more you freak out, the more you will make mistakes. Set aside 10 to 20 minutes a day for relaxation. Just make sure you do not multitask while you relax, like browsing the Internet while watching TV or texting while relaxing. It will not let you relax at all.
33

SPEND QUALITY TIME WITH LOVED ONES. If there is one important thing I will advise anyone who works from home, it is to spend quality time with your family. In case you are a work-at-home mom or dad, do not let the kids feel like they are competing for your attention. Put the phone out of reach when it is time to be with them, or keep them busy with creative activities while you are working. That way, they will not end up too clingy, which can be quite distracting. The truth is there are many drawbacks of working at home with children especially with young children. Just because you are around does not mean you are always available. Teach them "ground rules" about your home business so they will understand when to play with you and when to play by themselves. On the other hand, having a good relationship with your spouse is an important factor in productivity. [34]It is so easy to be always thinking about deadlines when you are at home without remembering that there is your spouse who also would enjoy your time and attention.

Work smarter, not harder. The work smarter, not harder approach is an old-age technique. Here are some tips to work smarter:

CREATE A "TO-DON'T LIST." Done with your to-do list? Why not come up with a list telling what you should not do for that day—answering unimportant phone calls, spending time on useless tasks, watching too much TV, and so on.

ACCEPT FAILURE. Failing is okay. As a freelancer, you have to understand that rejections and failures are a part of life. When a client rejects your work even after you gave your all, just think that this did not fit your needs perfectly either. There are times when the fit just is not right.

BE CONSISTENT. When you are consistent, it is way easier to build trust between clients. Being consistent also helps you realize that your client expects a lot from you. Knowing that somebody trusts you will motivate you to get things done and be more productive.

GET THE BAD STUFF OUT OF THE WAY. One way to stay motivated is to surround yourself with positivity so you have to make a conscious effort to get the bad stuff out of the way. We all have our share of defeats and disappointments in life. Whenever I encounter negative people (critics, complainers, and naysayers) in my work-at-home business, I just ask myself: Do I really have to deal with these people? Of course not! Wasting time, energy, and attention on things that do not really matter is a big no if you want to be more productive and happier at work.

BREAK YOUR GRAND IDEAS INTO BITE-SIZED PIECES. If you have great ideas that you want to achieve right away, break them in small parts and take baby steps to achieve them. Sometimes, we fail to do arduous tasks because we are anxious that it is too hard. Always remember, big successes are a pile of small actions. Do not be afraid to start small.

LEARN. Every day is a new opportunity to learn. Read wonderful tips from people on your career. Look for a summary of David Allen's Getting Things Done. Follow some productivity blogs and get inspiration from them. [35]

KNOW YOURSELF. Observe your behaviors and particular habits. List your strengths and weaknesses. This way you will realize what you have to improve.

GET DRESSED. Dressing up is one way to project professionalism. In my case, I do not work in my pajamas. It makes me feel like I do not work and I am still at home. John Stark, of Next Avenue, came up with ideas on how one should dress up working at home. His suggestions will apply to fashionistas as he gave some tidbits of how his work-at-home buddies dressed up during the fashion week. The fashion pieces are made up of coats, leg warmers, and skinny jeans. However, if you are living in a not-so-cold country, just choose anything that makes you more comfortable. Smart fabrics like cotton shirts and lose pants are good picks. [36]

WAKE UP AND JUST WRITE EVERYTHING YOU HAVE ON YOUR MIND. Science suggests that the best time to write is in the morning. It is the time of day when our prefrontal cortex is most active. If you are a creative writer, I suggest you work during mornings because it is when the creative mind is awake.

REMEMBER THAT YOU ARE STILL WORKING. You may not have a boss who watches everything you do, but it is not an excuse to stop working or have more breaks than what you should have.

GIVE A LITTLE REWARD FOR YOURSELF. Whenever I encounter demanding tasks that make me just want to sleep or eat, I remind myself of that little reward. I also learned that it is important to reward yourself when you are adopting a new habit. Charles Duhigg, author of The Power of Habit, talked about it in an interview with writer Chris Bailey.[37] In my case, it can be as simple as pampering myself after a long day of work. I take a hot bath or sometimes, I go to the spa to get a pedicure. One saying that motivates me is "no work, no money, and no reward." Moreover, it does not matter what the reward is. What is more important is that you truly enjoyed that reward.

TELL YOURSELF THAT YOU WILL ACCOMPLISH MORE TODAY. Remember the law of attraction? I apply it in every aspect of my life. When I find a task so challenging, I tell myself that it is going to be smooth-sailing as long as I give my all. The bottom line is to think positively, and you will get more done!

PLACE A PLANT NEAR YOUR DESK. Plants, when placed strategically, raises alertness by up to 70%. Some good choices are areca palms, which humidifies naturally; variegated snake plant, which purifies the air; and lemon balm which elevates one's mood. [38]

CHEW GUM. They say chewing gum boosts productivity. Some say it is just a myth. But one study in St. Lawrence University in New York suggested that chewing gum has positive cognitive effects.[39] Whether it is proven to boost productivity or not, chew a gum whenever you think that helps.

TRY THE "EAT-A-FROG TECHNIQUE."[40] The frog symbolizes the most unwanted task you have for that day. Henry Paulson, a businessman and author, said that the first thing he did every morning was the thing he was dreading the most that day. Eating a "frog" might be very difficult, but once you have completed that task you are dreading the most, you will feel better for accomplishing something.

SET TARGETS. For example, if you have to finish an article, tell yourself that you are not getting up for any reason until you have written at least half of it. Refuse to stop until you hit your target.

IDENTIFY YOUR PEAK TIMES. Craig Balantyne, a writer at Early to Rise, said we have that "Magic Time" of the day when our productivity triples. Do you hate early meetings?[41] Do you find it enjoyable to work after lunch? Or does your mind work best at night? It is time to determine your peak times. Are you a morning person or a night owl? In my case, I like working early, while others are still asleep, so I guess I am more of a morning person.

SET REALISTIC GOALS. It is of highest importance to set goals you can achieve. Making unrealistic goals can only result to high expectations that could even lead to depression. Aside from working hard and pushing your limits, the best way to get what you want is to set realistic goals.

Bonus Hacks

VISUALIZE. Imagine how you can offer your best self on that day. Spend at least 1o to 20 minutes "daydreaming" what you want to achieve on that day. After that, create an expectation in mind of all the things you have to do to make it happen. Visualization is also a good option if you want to meditate and relax your mind. Just close your eyes, dream of your favorite place, and unwind. Perhaps you should have a vision board close to you.

FOCUS ON RESULTS. I apply the Pareto technique when it comes to focusing on results. As mentioned earlier, Pareto is an 80/20 rule. To help you focus more on results, do the 20% things in life that bring you 80% of your happiness. As someone who works from home, the 20% you do is your job, and the 80% are your rewards. [42]

BLOG ABOUT YOUR ACHIEVEMENTS AND PERSONAL DEVELOPMENT. Some might say, "I do not want to blog about my achievements. It feels like bragging." If you are still in doubt how blogging can help you become more productive, here is why: it is one way to make a public commitment. It promises others that you will finish or you will accomplish something.

TELL OTHER PEOPLE ABOUT YOUR GOALS. Making public commitments is another way to get things done. Do it by declaring that you will get something done on a specific time. This way, you will be forced to pull it off.

BE INSPIRED BY SMALL SUCCESSES. You do not have to be a total achiever. If you accomplished at least two of your goals in one day, then it is enough. At the end of the day, success is still about liking what you do.

CHANGE YOUR MOOD. Successful people are givers and not takers of positive energy. Did you wake up feeling optimistic about work? Having a positive outlook helps you keep on track. I remember one Wall Street Journal article which says "Put on happy face. Seriously." The article is basically about the connection of employees' mood to their performances. What if you work at home? How will you reset the button when things go awry? If your bad mood is recurring, take a few minutes to watch a funny sitcom or YouTube videos.[43]

ENJOY WHAT YOU DO. If you enjoy what you do, you will find yourself more productive. Working from home can be very wonderful so just enjoy it. Appreciate the perks of it rather than worry about all the distractions at home. Besides, it is impossible to find happiness in a career you do not enjoy. But aside from enjoying what you do, it is more important to do not just the tasks you like. After all, each job has its boring moments. It is not always "fun stuff" even if you enjoy what you are doing.

TAKE A FIELD TRIP. When you get tired of working in your office, take a trip to the living room or deck and enjoy your new surroundings. I like to plan to work at a coffee shop two times a week. This way, I have some great coffee and a change of scenery. It gets me out the house, and I even meet new people there.

TAKE YOUR BATHROOM TRIPS. I play a game with myself that just might prove to be a true test for my kidneys. I try to see how much I can get completed on a task before I take a bathroom break. Being a former middle school teacher, I am very cognizant of 'holding it' while waiting for my students to leave at the end of class. I do not suggest this for the kidney challenged; however, it really helps me ramp up my typing.

FAVORITE APPS AND SOFTWARE. I love using Typeitin and other WavGet products. I cannot live without Grammarly

And the most important thing of all, **IMPLEMENT EVERYTHING YOU KNOW ABOUT PRODUCTIVITY THAT WILL FIT YOUR STYLE.** They say it is easier said than done. However, if you never implement the things you learn, all the words and incentives are just a waste of time. Knowing it all without doing it all is not going to help you get out of the home office and get you more down time.

There is a relationship between productivity and motivation. It is simple; when one is motivated, the task will be completed by whatever it takes. Motivation does not just happen. It has to start with a goal. Now, what is your goal? Are your goals enough to motivate you?

CONCLUSION

There is no magic pill for productivity.

It is all about managing *effectively all the resources you have: time, energy, knowledge, and work environment.* It is about learning to cope with distractions. It is finding time for the important things. There is no shortcut in this thing we call "productivity." But one thing is for sure: productivity has to start with intention. It is about the desire to work. It is moving toward accomplishing the things you want to get done. No tool, no matter how good it is, can give you productivity—you have to be willing to get started.

We all have our meanings of productivity. What is yours? Do you find yourself productive today?

I hope you enjoyed reading! Carpe diem.

Deb Gilbert

ABOUT THE AUTHOR

Thank you for purchasing this Kindle Book. For updates and more information, check out: www.gilbertedservices.com
My other books:

If you are a Baby Boomer and are either planning your retirement or living your retirement, you will want to join my blog, web site, and Facebook group Retirement Baby Boomer Style.

Web Site: http://www.retirebabyboomerstyle.com/
Facebook Group:
https://www.facebook.com/groups/retiredbabyboomers/
Blog: http://retirebabyboomerstyle.net

For more information on Deb Gilbert, please join her at www.gilbertedservices.com

Deb Gilbert

ENDNOTES

3 http://24hoursbetter.com/_truncated

4 http://www.jameshbyrd.com/use-excel-to-create-accurate-project-estimates/_truncated

5 http://www.lifehack.org/articles/productivity/how-to-use-parkinsons-law-to-your-advantage.html

6 http://www.sermoncentral.com/sermons/take-a-break-denn-guptill-sermon-on-sabbath-150377.asp

7 http://www.makeuseof.com/tag/how-to-become-a-chrome-power-user-part-1-master-the-keyboard/

8 http://jamesclear.com/how-to-stop-procrastinating

9 http://www.cbsnews.com/news/apply-the-80-20-rule-to-weed-out-gross-inefficiencies/

10 https://www.americanexpress.com/us/small-business/openforum/articles/productivity-tips-from-incredibly-busy-entrepreneurs/

11 http://news.bbc.co.uk/2/hi/uk_news/4471607.stm

12 http://news.nationalpost.com/2014/09/15/dr-aw-sleep-why-its-essential-how-a-lack-of-it-can-shrink-your-brain-and-what-to-do-if-you-cant-get-enough-hint-its-not-a-drug/

13 http://blog.mass.gov/publichealth/mass-in-motion/trouble-in-the-sleep-department-8-tips-for-better-sleep/

14 http://tinybuddha.com/blog/5-ways-get-energized-motivated-feel-lazy/

15 http://pom.sagepub.com/content/33/2/173.abstract

16 http://www.designinfographics.com/food-infographics/coffee-at-work-a-pick-me-up-for-workers-careers

17 http://businessjournal.gallup.com/content/23146/too-many-interruptions-work.aspx

18 http://thefreelancepinoy.com/2011/09/a-more-productive-freelancer/#.VB5xjBawStY

19 http://pomodorotechnique.com/

20 http://www.makeuseof.com/tag/sunday-4-tips-plan-balance-work-week/

21 http://alizul2.blogspot.com/2014/01/infographic-how-office-tech-and-decor.html

22 http://homeguides.sfgate.com/paint-colors-calming-make-room-big-46716.html

23 http://en.paperblog.com/you-do-not-have-to-do-everything-on-your-own-extract-from-my-new-ebook-358960/www.briantracy.com/blog/time-management/plan-ahead-and-increase-productivity/

24 http://en.paperblog.com/you-do-not-have-to-do-everything-on-your-own-extract-from-my-new-ebook-358960/

25 http://www.virgin.com/richard-branson/top-10-tips-for-making-lists

26 http://www.everydaykanban.com/what-is-kanban/

27 http://www.quora.com/Time-Management/How-does-one-manage-time-more-effectively

28 http://vorkspace.com/blog/index.php/6-tips-stay-focused-working-home/

29 http://jamesclear.com/new-habit

30 http://universaljourney.co.uk/mindfulness-businesses/

31 http://www.depts.ttu.edu/upwardbound/books/the-7-habits-ofhighly-effective-people.pdf

32 http://www.nytimes.com/2013/02/10/opinion/sunday/relax-youll-be-more-productive.html?pagewanted=all

33 http://www.drwayneandersen.com/2013/03/18/stress-reduction-the-relaxation-response/

34 http://myfinancemoney.com/the-downside-of-working-at-home-with-children/

35 http://gettingthingsdone.com/

36 http://www.nextavenue.org/staff/john-stark

37 http://charlesduhigg.com/

38 http://blog.htc.ca/2014/04/23/decorate-for-doing-workplace-decor-that-works/

39 http://www.dailymail.co.uk/news/article-2072816/Chewing-gum-tests-improves-scores.html

40 http://www.toodledo.com/info/frog.php

41 http://www.earlytorise.com/identify-the-magic-time-to-get-more-done/

42 http://management.about.com/cs/generalmanagement/a/Pareto081202.htm

43 http://online.wsj.com/news/articles/SB10001424052970203388804576612943738516996

Made in the USA
Lexington, KY
20 January 2018